Jane
LYNCH

ACTRESS AND ACTIVIST

REMARKABLE
LGBTQ
LIVES™

Jane
LYNCH

ACTRESS AND ACTIVIST

JENNIFER LANDAU

ROSEN
PUBLISHING®
New York

Published in 2015 by The Rosen Publishing Group, Inc.
29 East 21st Street, New York, NY 10010

First Edition

Library of Congress Cataloging-in-Publication Data

Landau, Jennifer, 1961–
Jane Lynch: actress and activist/Jennifer Landau.—
First edition.
     pages cm.—(Remarkable LGBTQ lives)
Includes bibliographical references and index.
ISBN 978-1-4777-7901-9 (library bound)
1. Lynch, Jane, 1960-—Juvenile literature. 2. Ac-
tors—United States—Biography—Juvenile literature.
I. Title.
PN2287.L95L35 2014
792.02'8092—dc23
[B]
                                        2014007059

Manufactured in China

CONTENTS

INTRO

On September 4, 2013, Jane Lynch received a star on the Hollywood Walk of Fame in Los Angeles, California. In an interview with a reporter from the E! television network, Lynch said getting her star was so amazing that she had never dared to dream that such a thing could happen.

Many dreams have come true for Jane Lynch. She titled her memoir

DUCTION

Happy Accidents because of her deep apprecia-
tion for the role luck has played in her success.
For example, Lynch auditioned for a Frosted Flakes
commercial, not knowing that the director was
filmmaker Christopher Guest. Her appearance in
that cereal commercial led to a major role in Guest's
next film. Of course, if Lynch's enormous talent
hadn't impressed him, that bit of luck would have
gotten her nowhere.

After years of working in theater, film, and television, Lynch has now reached icon status. Her
portrayal of Sue Sylvester on *Glee* has led to an
Emmy Award, a Golden Globe Award, her own
Hollywood star, and even a mass-produced Sue
Sylvester Halloween costume! She is more sought
after than ever, hosting a prime-time game show and
events such as NBC's 2013 New Year's broadcast
and the 2014 Directors Guild Awards.

It was only after years of
hard work as a stage, film,
and television actress
that Jane Lynch earned
her star on the Hollywood
Walk of Fame.

Although Lynch struggled to come to terms with being a lesbian, she is now not only at ease with her own sexuality but also a strong supporter of many lesbian, gay, bisexual, transgender, and questioning (LGBTQ) organizations. She has used her considerable fame to raise awareness on issues such as marriage equality, the bullying of LGBTQ teens, and providing food for those dealing with AIDs and other illnesses.

Lynch is a beloved performer, and although most people know her sexual orientation, she is known for much more than that. This is true for an increasing number of celebrities, including actor Jim Parsons, broadcaster Robin Roberts, and diver Tom Daley, all of whom have "come out" in low-key ways, rather than with cover stories in major magazines.

Attitudes toward the LGBTQ population are changing, too. According to a 2013 Gallup poll, 52 percent of Americans support marriage equality. More and more states are legalizing gay marriage, and the Supreme Court ruled on two cases that helped move the cause forward. This progress does not mean that discrimination against the LGBTQ community is over. It does suggest, however, that celebrities such as Jane Lynch can have a tremendous impact not only on their own community, but also on the general public. Sue Sylvester would expect nothing less.

CHAPTER 1

DIFFERENT FROM THE OTHER GIRLS

While promoting *Happy Accidents* on the late-night show *Chelsea Lately*, Jane Lynch said that the idea of writing her memoir came from speeches she had given to various organizations. One of these organizations was the Human Rights Campaign (HRC), an advocacy group that "strives to end discrimination against LGBT citizens and realize a nation that achieves fundamental fairness and equality for all," according to its mission statement on its website, www.hrc.org.

On October 10, 2009, Lynch gave a speech at the HRC's 13th Annual National Dinner in Washington, D.C., at which President Barack Obama gave the keynote, or main, address. During her short speech, Lynch joked that she was "not an activist by nature" but a "complainer by nature...a media-bloated arm-chair warrior." On a more serious note, she stated that when the LGBTQ community stands "in the truth of who we are, our example is so powerful."

Although Lynch is now open about her sexual orientation and works to support LGBTQ causes—among other issues—this was not always the case. It took her many years to stand in *her* own truth and accept who she was, not only as a lesbian, but also as a performer, friend, and partner.

A HAPPY HOME

Jane Lynch was born on July 14, 1960, in Dolton, Illinois, a small town south of Chicago. Her father, Frank, was a banker and her mother, Eileen, a secretary at Arthur Andersen, a large accounting firm. In her memoir, Lynch describes her Irish father as a man who loved to joke around, and his zany humor delighted—and no doubt influenced—his daughter. Her father would rub suntan lotion all over his nearly bald head and then use conditioner to smooth out what few strands of hair he had left.

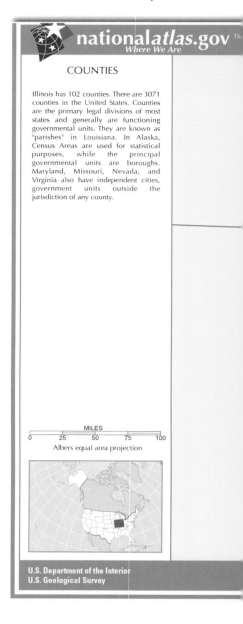

nationalatlas.gov ™
Where We Are

COUNTIES

Illinois has 102 counties. There are 3071 counties in the United States. Counties are the primary legal divisions of most states and generally are functioning governmental units. They are known as "parishes" in Louisiana. In Alaska, Census Areas are used for statistical purposes, while the principal governmental units are boroughs. Maryland, Missouri, Nevada, and Virginia also have independent cities, government units outside the jurisdiction of any county.

MILES
0   25   50   75   100
Albers equal area projection

U.S. Department of the Interior
U.S. Geological Survey

Jane's mother, Eileen, was also funny, but often unintentionally so. According to *Happy Accidents*, her mother was a bit absentminded and rarely the first to get a joke. Although she might not have

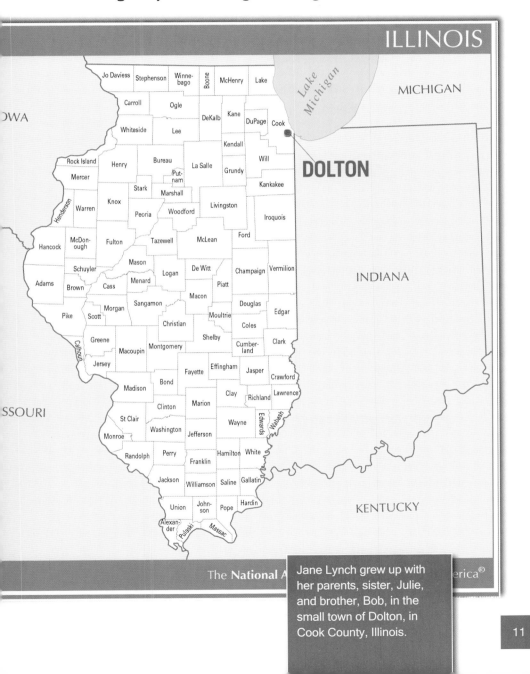

ILLINOIS

Jane Lynch grew up with her parents, sister, Julie, and brother, Bob, in the small town of Dolton, in Cook County, Illinois.

been as quick-witted as others in the family, Jane's mother was a strong woman with little time for foolish behavior or show-offs. In her memoir, Lynch jokes that her mother should have shown her daughter a little patience as she was a "foolish, bragging show-off," but Jane was dearly loved nonetheless.

Every year, Jane's mother and father would perform in *Port O' Call*, a show put on by the local parish church. For this show, different rooms were decorated to look like an Irish tavern, a German cabaret, and other locations around the world. The audience would move from room to room to take in the show, while Jane was thrilled to watch everything that was happening backstage with the performers. Just being in their company made her feel like she was in show business.

DARK ENERGY

Despite this excitement and the comfort of being raised in a stable and happy home, Lynch was often filled with a "dark energy," as she writes in her memoir. The energy would build up so much that the only way to release it was to have a total meltdown and end up kicking and screaming on the floor, certain that no one understood her.

In the commencement address at Smith College, Lynch encouraged the graduates to embrace whatever life brought their way rather than acting out of fear.

13

As she said in her commencement address to the Smith College graduating class of 2012, she often felt "alien in the world and in my own body" as a child. A large part of this feeling was because she was certain that she should have been born a boy.

As a kid, Jane loved to dress up as a hobo or pirate on Halloween and would even try on her father's clothes when nobody was looking. Her younger brother, Bob, had little interest in sports, while Jane longed to play ball with her father and do other things considered boyish.

Jane was not particularly close to Bob, who was quiet and shy, or to her older sister Julie, a girly-girl who loved to play with dolls. A typical middle child, Jane fought for attention and would do just about anything to get it. At home, she'd answer the phone and speak baby talk to whomever was calling, which always got a laugh. Jane could only hear out of her left ear—likely due to a childhood illness—and when she was eight, she found out that, unlike her, most people could hear out of both ears. Rather than being upset, Jane was happy to get this news because she craved attention so much that she looked at any chance to seem different, especially in relation to her brother and sister, as a positive thing.

KEEPING A SECRET

Jane was twelve when she realized that she was different from most other girls because she was gay. She didn't know the word until she heard two classmates talking about the men they saw holding hands on the beach in Florida. They said the word "gay" with a tone of disgust, and at the time, Jane not only felt that she was the same as those men on the beach, but also that being gay was perverted and had to be kept secret from other people.

One of the things that makes Jane Lynch such a likeable public figure is her honesty. Even as an out-and-proud mature adult, she has had to deal with her own traces of homophobia. When a person is homophobic, he or she has an aversion to or an irrational fear of homosexuality, which leads to discrimination against the LGBTQ community. Although Lynch is hardly one to discriminate against her own community, in 2011 she told Judith Newman of the *New York Times* that whenever she saw a feminine-acting man on television, she thought, "'Couldn't you butch it up a little?' I want us to make ourselves more palatable to the world." Lynch later considered her expectation that LGBTQ people conduct themselves in a manner more in keeping with stereotypical gender roles as a generational issue because Lara Embry, her wife at the time—the two divorced in January 2014—was nine years younger and had no such concerns.

Lynch's view that such concerns are generational is supported by statistics. A 2013 survey by the Pew Research Center found that, in the United States, 70 percent of people ages eighteen to twenty-nine were accepting of homosexuality compared to 52 percent of people over the age of fifty. Even in countries that oppose gay rights, attitudes are changing among the younger generation. In Lebanon, 80 percent of the population rejected homosexuality. However, almost 30 percent of those twenty-nine or younger said that homosexuality should be accepted compared to only 10 percent of people fifty or older.

DISCOVERING THEATER

In 2010, Lynch and Lara Embry made a video for the It Gets Better Project. According to a statement on its website, the project was created to help LGBT youth through their growing up years by showing "the levels of happiness, potential, and positivity their lives will reach—if they can just get through their teen years."

The It Gets Better Project is the brainchild of author and columnist Dan Savage. Savage and his partner, Terry Miller, posted a video on YouTube as a message of hope for young people facing harassment. Over time, more than fifty thousand people created supportive

videos, including celebrities, average citizens, and members of the LGBTQ community and its straight allies.

For their work on the It Gets Better Project, Terry Miller (*left*) and Dan Savage received the Governors Award at the 2012 Creative Arts Emmys.

A. A. Milne wrote the play *The Ugly Duckling*, based on the fairy tale by Hans Christian Andersen. In a high school play, Jane played the part of the king who plots to have his ugly daughter marry a prince from distant lands.

In her video on the It Gets Better site, Lynch talks about feeling as if she had a disease when she realized she was gay. She felt very alone and wished that she understood that her life would improve over time. She encourages LGBTQ youth to "hang in there and know that there are people in this world who love you for who you are." Part of what helped her, she states, was being involved in theater, an activity that attracted a lot of LGBTQ students.

In high school, Jane was deeply closeted, meaning she told no one about her attraction to other girls. For a number of years, she didn't even acknowledge these feelings to herself because she saw being gay as a disease she suffered. She slowly found her way to the world of acting, which would eventually help her. In her freshman year of high school, she got the part of the king in *The Ugly Duckling*. She often would be cast in roles that were originally written for men, in part because she reached her full height of 6 feet (1.8 meters) by the time she was sixteen years old.

Jane was thrilled to get the part but was so nervous during rehearsals that she froze, unable to continue. She left the production, earning a reputation as a quitter. As she told Margy Rochlin of *More* magazine, it was her intense need to succeed as an actress that tripped her up: "It was as if I was walking up to my destiny, and I got scared and turned around and joined the tennis team."

SUPPORT FROM THE WHITE HOUSE

Among those who have made an It Gets Better video are President Barack Obama and, in a separate video, several members of the White House staff. In his 2010 video, President Obama spoke about students who had committed suicide after being bullied about their sexual orientation. He considers these deaths heartbreaking and states that no one should have to put up with bullying or "feel so alone or desperate that they feel they have nowhere to turn."

President Obama is candid about being bullied as a young adult (this bullying was due to his appearance and unusual name, not his sexual orientation) and considering suicide. He credits a coworker with offering the support that helped him see a way out. President Obama states that LGBTQ youths dealing with bullying or other issues deserve the same level of support.

Inspired by President Obama's message, LGBTQ members of the White House staff made a video in which they discuss dealing with bullying, low self-esteem, and loneliness as young people. They state that during their darkest days they couldn't imagine leading full and happy lives, yet they persevered to do just that. As Ellie Schafer, director of the White House Visitors Office, says in the It Gets Better video, "Don't let anyone tell you that you're a second-class citizen or that you don't deserve the best in life, because you do."

LIFE OF THE PARTY

In high school, Jane was the class clown, which made her popular. She was not a serious student but instead liked to party with her friends. Much of this partying involved alcohol, and Jane started drinking in her freshman year of high school. At first she drank a beer every once in a while, but by her junior year, the drinking became a nightly event.

Jane went to high school in the 1970s, and in her neighborhood at that time, drinking was part of the overall culture. This didn't make her drinking any less problematic, however, and the problem would only get worse over time. "I suffered over my drinking," she told comedian Joy Behar on *The Joy Behar Show* in 2011. "I suffered over the fact that I lived for it, that I lived each day to get to the part of the day where I could drink."

In high school, Jane goofed around and partied, but she still often felt like she was on the outside looking in. A lot of her isolation had to do with her romantic feelings toward her female classmates. Jane had crushes on many different girls and would dream of rescuing those she thought needed her help. As an adult, Lynch realized that it was she who needed saving from the feelings of shame she felt about her sexual orientation and the loneliness of hiding it.

These feelings would have a great impact on how she lived her life once she became a well-known actress. In 2012, when she accepted the Bill of Rights Award from the American Civil Liberties Union (ACLU) of Southern California, she stated that she wasn't always "keen on having faceless people know something as private as my sexual orientation." However, her role on *Glee* had made her someone young people looked up to, and remembering her own struggles, she joked that "at the tender age of fifty," she felt ready to serve as a role model for LGBTQ youths.

A LIFE IN THE THEATER

One of the many organizations that Jane Lynch supports is the Adopt the Arts program, which aims to return the arts to schools struggling with limited budgets. Adopt the Arts chooses a public school and then gives that school everything it needs to maintain an arts program, including a curriculum to follow, instruments, and art supplies.

Lynch attends a party in support of Adopt the Arts, alongside its founder, drummer Matt Sorum (*left*), and actor Johnathon Schaech.

23

In a video about Adopt the Arts, Lynch says that singing in the choir and acting in plays were the highlights of her high school experience because she felt most herself when expressing herself creatively.

As a high school student, once she overcame her stage fright, Jane dove into the world of acting and singing as a way to deal with her feelings of shame and isolation about being gay. On stage, she felt that the things that made her different could be hidden and that she was worthy of the attention she received from the audience.

A PLACE TO BELONG

During Jane's high school years, black students were integrated into her school, which had a white population. The black kids were brought in from other neighborhoods by bus, and this action caused a lot of tension, with riots in the school and police called in to keep the peace. Much as in the TV show *Glee* on which she would later star, the choral room in her high school was a place where kids from all different backgrounds worked in harmony. No matter their race or to what clique they belonged—there were

cheerleaders, football players, and nerds in chorus—
all the students got along as they sang together.

Despite her reputation as a quitter after leaving her
school's production of *The Ugly Duckling*, Jane was

This photograph shows opening night at a Broadway production of *Godspell*. Lynch performed in the play during her high school years.

able to get some plum parts. In *Arsenic and Old Lace*, she played a male police officer, and in *The Brick and the Rose*, she played a male tomboy. In her interview in *More* magazine, she acknowledged that she was hard to cast: "I was still kind of a tomboy. I didn't look like a boy or a girl. I didn't carry myself as one thing or another. I was just stuck."

When her theater arts class put on a production of *Godspell* during her senior year, however, she played a very feminine character. Jane's character was the hussy, a woman with loose morals who wore a feather boa draped around her neck. Jane was elated to be in the play and to share in the excitement of bringing *Godspell* to life. Although she felt nervous performing, she was filled with

CAN GAY ACTORS PLAY STRAIGHT ROLES?

In an article titled "Playing It Straight," posted on the *Newsweek* website on April 26, 2010, journalist Ramin Setoodeh, who is openly gay, shared his belief that when straight actors played gay characters, the performance was usually successful, while gay actors were rarely convincing when playing straight characters. He believed that an actor's background had a strong impact on how an audience viewed that actor in a role. For Setoodeh, this meant that a gay actor had a harder time coming across as straight, especially when he or she was playing a romantic lead.

Although most in the acting community criticized Setoodeh's views as homophobic, Jane Lynch didn't think the writer was totally off base. In a 2011 interview with the website AfterElton, Lynch agreed that because most people are straight and movie and TV studios want the audience to fall in love with the lead romantic characters, only straight actors could be used for the time being.

Although Lynch didn't believe that she had been discriminated against for being a lesbian, she thought this was because she was a character actor, not a leading lady. She also thought she could get away with playing a straight romantic lead because she was older. Hollywood, however, wanted the young Romeo and Juliet types to be played by straight actors. In the interview, she argued that it was the studios driving this trend because they were more concerned with making money than trying to change the way things work in show business.

When Ramin Setoodeh wrote a *Newsweek* article in 2010 stating that gay actors were rarely convincing playing straight characters, his comments were widely criticized by both the acting and LGBTQ communities.

a joy she had never experienced before. She had discovered the path she wanted to follow in her professional life.

A TRUE FRIEND

In her youth, deeply troubled by her attraction to girls, Jane tried dating boys, telling herself that she should be enjoying her time with them. Going on dates with boys was clearly difficult for someone who, years later, would describe herself as "really, really gay" with "no interest in men sexually" during a 2011 interview on *The Joy Behar Show.*

Along with her interest in performing, Jane's friendship with a boy, a high school classmate named Chris Patrick, offered great solace. Chris was gay, and although the two of them didn't discuss this fact at first, Jane was taken by how comfortable Chris was in his own skin. If Jane was one to follow the rules, Chris was rebellious, a prankster who loved nothing more than to make her laugh. He would even throw himself down the school stairs, his books flying everywhere, to get Jane to crack up.

Chris egged Jane on, encouraging her to cut class one day and go out for soda and fries instead. At the restaurant, they used cigarette ashes to make crosses on each other's foreheads and then told the campus police that they had gone to Mass. Jane relaxed around Chris because she could see aspects of her own personality in this kind, nonjudgmental friend.

Unlike Jane, Chris felt no shame about his sexual orientation and started visiting gay bars on the weekends. Unable to deal with her own gayness at the time, she stayed in denial about Chris being gay, too. A rift in their relationship developed when Chris started spending time alone with another gay boy at school. She felt like she'd been dumped and was angry at being forced to confront Chris's sexual orientation when she was so terrified of her own.

Jane also worried that others at school might assume she was a lesbian because her close friend was gay. She pushed Chris away and spent the end of her high school days feeling hurt and alone.

A TASTE OF SUCCESS

Jane had never been a particularly impressive student. Beyond theater and chorus, she had little interest in school and was not keen on going to college. However, that was what other high school graduates did, so in 1978, she headed to Illinois State University, where the B and C students in her school went to college. Illinois State was in a city named Normal, Illinois, and Lynch found that fact amusing, especially given how different she felt from others in her age group.

Lynch's mother wanted her to major in something that might lead to good job prospects, such as mass communications. Like many parents, she worried that a life in the theater would offer no financial security for her daughter.

Luckily for Lynch, the entry-level communications course was closed by the time she went to register, so she started taking acting classes. Another stroke of luck was that even though she was a lackluster student, Lynch had managed to get into a school that had a great theater department. Recent graduates of the program had gone on to form the well-respected Steppenwolf Theatre Company, based in Chicago.

Incoming freshmen were not allowed to try out for plays, but during her second semester, Lynch snagged a role in *Lysistrata*, a comedy by Aristophanes, a writer in ancient Greece. *Lysistrata* is a fictional tale about a group of women who withhold sex from their husbands until the men agree to settle the Peloponnesian War (431–404 BCE) peacefully.

At Illinois State, the play was rewritten with a Southern theme, and Lynch played the role of a country bumpkin named Karmenia of Kornith. It was rare for a freshman to get a speaking part in a play, which was a testament to her talent.

Lynch decided to play Karmenia as openly lesbian, an interesting choice given how closeted she herself was. There were many closeted gay people in the theater department and only one out lesbian, whom Lynch refers to as a butch lesbian in *Happy Accidents*, meaning she dressed and acted in a masculine way. Lynch was still so afraid to admit her own attraction toward women that she avoided this classmate.

THE DIVA

A role in *Gypsy*, the musical about stripper Gypsy Rose Lee, was a turning point for Lynch. She expected to be in the chorus but was given the role of another stripper named Electra. It was an elaborate production and gave Lynch a taste of what it would be like to have a part in a Broadway musical. While trying to lose her Chicago-area accent, Lynch started speaking in American Standard English, which her family found quite impressive and a little bit alienating.

Lynch was also quick to criticize her classmates if she thought their acting was not up to snuff. At the time, she was shocked that her behavior turned people off, but she later realized that she was attacking others because she felt so inadequate herself. She also mistook her talent as an actor for brilliance.

During her senior year in college, Lynch had her first romantic relationship with a woman—an openly gay professor ten years her senior. Dating this woman was frightening for Lynch because it confirmed that her

Natalie Wood, shown here, starred as stripper Gypsy Rose Lee in the 1962 film *Gypsy*. While in college, Lynch appeared in the stage version of *Gypsy*, playing fellow stripper Electra.

lesbianism was a reality. The two had a rocky relationship, with Lynch wanting to be with her girlfriend one
minute and then as far away from her as possible the
next. She had such a difficult time processing all the
emotions of being with another woman that the two
parted ways.

In the midst of this turmoil, Lynch reached out
to her high school friend Chris Patrick. She told him
that she was gay and asked him to forgive her for
pushing him away because she couldn't deal with her
own sexuality. Patrick was quick to point out that he
knew she was gay. He was also quick to forgive.

AN ADVANCED EDUCATION

Lynch was still uncomfortable with her sexuality and
had not come completely out of the closet, but she
was fully committed to her acting career. She went
on to graduate school at Cornell University in Ithaca,
New York. Cornell was an Ivy League school on the
East Coast, and coming from a small Midwestern
town, Lynch felt very out of place there.

Feeling inadequate compared to her peers and
conflicted about her sexuality, Lynch threw herself
into her work as an actor. Playing roles that were
far different from her allowed Lynch a welcome
escape. Unfortunately, alcohol offered an escape
that was far less healthy. Lynch would drink
heavily, an entire six-pack at times, to get

Having grown up in a small Midwestern town, Lynch felt overwhelmed when she first arrived at Cornell University, a sprawling Ivy League institution in Ithaca, New York.

temporary relief from her psychological pain.

She also went back to her diva ways, letting her classmates know that nothing they did was good enough. In truth, Lynch doubted her own abilities, but she was so "fundamentally broken," as she says in her memoir, that all she could do was lash out. She even made her family miserable, complaining every step of the way during a rare vacation together.

After *Happy Accidents* was published in 2011, Lynch gave an interview to a reporter from the *Advocate* and stated that she hoped the message of her book was to "[t]rust your life and trust where you are right now." Lynch was able to reach this equanimity not when she achieved fame, but when she began to believe in her talent as an actor and fully embrace her sexual orientation.

When Lynch moved to New York City after graduating from Cornell in 1984, she had yet to reach this balance. She couldn't find acting work and felt adrift in a city that was far less safe than it is today. The only place Lynch felt happy was at the Duplex, a small cabaret theater where she would listen to Broadway singers and then take her turn at the microphone at about four o'clock in the morning. She was drinking heavily and could not get in sync with a city that seemed to overwhelm her. After only nine months in New York, Lynch moved back to Illinois.

CHAPTER 3

A WORKING ACTOR

Although Lynch's parents were happy to have her back home, her mother encouraged her to get a steady job because acting was such an unreliable profession. Lynch agreed to apply for a secretarial position at the accounting firm where her mother worked, but she

When in her mid-twenties, Lynch appeared in Shakespeare's *The Comedy of Errors* at Chicago's Civic Opera House. This picture shows a production of the play at New York's Delacorte Theater in Central Park.

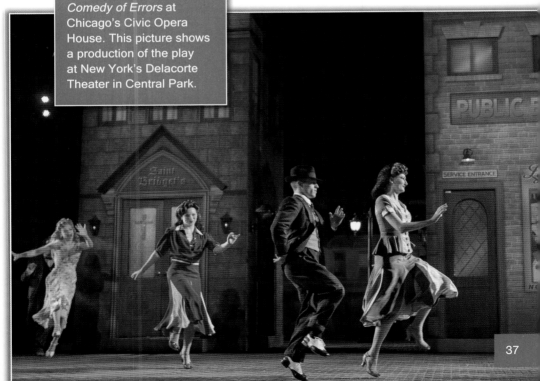

failed the English test. A job answering phones at the Civic Opera House in Chicago seemed ideal until she got a role in an outdoor production of Shakespeare's *The Comedy of Errors.* The part meant she had to quit her job, but when she told her employer this news, they fired her, greatly upsetting Lynch. She viewed it as a rejection, and increasingly dependent on alcohol, she drank far too much to deal with her feelings.

Lynch was a hit in the play, but a flop backstage, alienating the cast with her snobbish behavior. Although Lynch believed that she had some valid points in her criticism of her cast mates, she had zero tact when it came to discussing their work. She complained about everything, including the color of paint used to decorate the sets. Not surprisingly, when she quit the production, her fellow actors seemed more relieved than disappointed.

AMERICA'S SHOPPING PLACE

Lynch's next job was about as different from Shakespeare as one could imagine. In 1987, at the age of twenty-seven, Lynch began hosting *America's Shopping Place*, a home shopping program. The show was live, so the hosts had to be quick on their feet as they fielded calls from viewers and described the huge range of products. Lynch loved being on television and trading jokes with her cohost, but the executives in charge didn't think she was cute or feminine enough to serve as a permanent host for the program. She was put in the awkward position of having to host the show with women who were auditioning to be her replacement.

America's Shopping Place earned Lynch enough money to both rent an apartment in Chicago and buy a used car. She'd work all night, and then go through a six-pack of beer in the early hours of the next day, finishing off the beer as she watched tapes of herself on the show. Lynch's unhealthy way of living, including her dependence on alcohol to numb her pain and disappointment, was taking a heavy toll on both her mind and her body.

THE SECOND CITY

Despite Lynch's struggles, she never lost sight of her goal to be a working actor. She auditioned for the Second City, the famed improvisational (improv) group where Tina Fey, Amy Poehler, Steve Carell, and many others got their start. In improv comedy, there is no script. The actors make things up as they go along, playing off each other to create unique—and hopefully funny—sketches. As Lynch describes it in her Smith commencement speech, the basis of improv is "YES, AND." This means that no matter what your fellow actor comes up with, you expand on it, rather than shut him or her down. For example, if the actor cups his or her hands and pretends to be

Like the members of the Second City shown here, Lynch performed sketch comedy with the Chicago-based improvisational group.

collecting money out of a slot machine, you don't say, "Money? What are you talking about? Your hands are empty!" because that leaves nowhere to go. However, if you take what the actor is doing and expand on it ("I knew our luck was going to change. Now we can buy that yogurt shop!"), the sketch can move forward because you've created a "YES, AND" situation.

In 1987, Lynch was cast in the touring company of the Second City and traveled throughout the country with other cast members in a twelve-person van. This group performed "best of" sketches that had been developed on the main stage in Chicago. The work suited Lynch because, as she told

Elle magazine, "I loved sketch comedy, but I was never really good at the improv. I was never that good at finding the joke." Unlike other jobs, Lynch got along great with her fellow actors, and she felt lucky to be part of the group.

Occasionally, Lynch would substitute for a player on the main stage in Chicago. She took her job as an understudy seriously, watching the show every night to be prepared in case she was asked to perform. Expecting her hard work to result in a permanent spot on the main stage, she approached the producer, who made it clear that she would never be a member of the main company.

Lynch was heartbroken and left the Second City for good. This slight, along with being overlooked during her time on *America's Shopping Place*, made Lynch realize that she had a bad habit of going out of her way to please people who barely had her on their radar. Then when she didn't get the praise that she thought she deserved, she felt bitter.

BECOMING A BRADY

Not long after Lynch left the Second City, she was cast in a series of plays at the Steppenwolf Theatre, the group founded by several Illinois

Lynch *(top row, center)* felt a real kinship with her castmates in *The Real Live Brady Bunch*, a word-for-word recreation of the popular 1960s sitcom.

State University alumni. Along with performing at Steppenwolf, Lynch spent the next several years working as a commercial actor and voice-over artist. In voice-over work, the actor serves as a kind of narrator in TV and radio ads, movie trailers, and other projects. Lynch was willing to take any job she was offered, including a role in a 1988 super-low-budget film called *Taxi Killer* that never saw the light of day.

In 1990, Lynch joined a show called *The Real Live Brady Bunch*, a word-for-word reenactment of the popular sixties sitcom about a widow with three daughters who marries a widower with three sons. Lynch played Carol Brady, the mother, and loved working on the show, finding comfort in being part of a "perfect" family that resolved every issue quickly, even if that family was fictional. To everyone's surprise, *The Real Live Brady Bunch* was a big hit, with positive reviews and ticket lines down the block.

A SERIOUS PROBLEM

Although Lynch felt at ease performing in *The Real Live Brady Bunch,* she still had issues complicating her life. High on the list was her heavy consumption of alcohol. She wasn't so dysfunctional that she missed shows or forgot to pay her bills, but she had killer hangovers that she'd tried to head off by abusing over-the-counter medications that made her drowsy. After a time, however, even that stopped working.

Lynch's friend Chris Patrick had been a much heavier drinker than Lynch was, and he had been sober for years. One night in 1991, while on the phone with Patrick, Lynch realized the destructive role that alcohol played in her life. She poured the glass of wine she was drinking down the sink. It was the last drink she ever had.

BACK IN NEW YORK

In fall 1991, *The Real Live Brady Bunch* moved to New York City for a run at the Village Gate nightclub. Lynch hoped that her experience would be more positive than her last stay, when she ended up running home to Illinois. Although she loved being in the show, she still felt like an outsider among her fellow actors. Instead of sharing an apartment, she ended up living at a residence run by the Salvation Army. The Parkside Evangeline was a female-only residence and made Lynch feel like she was living in a convent.

It seems hard to reconcile the outgoing, outspoken Jane Lynch people have come to know with the lonely and isolated woman she was in her early thirties. Lynch was uncomfortable with intimacy and so disheartened during the day that she'd take over-the-counter medications that made her drowsy—a crutch she'd yet

While performing *The Real Live Brady Bunch* in New York in the early nineties, Lynch lived alone at the Parkside Evangeline, a women's residence. Although she loved acting in the show, Lynch still viewed herself as an outsider.

to give up—and sleep for hours just to pass the time before her nightly performance.

One night after a show, some of Lynch's cast mates were smoking marijuana. When she'd

A FALLEN FRIEND

Since achieving stardom, Jane Lynch has been open about her struggles with substance abuse. She understands how difficult it can be to stay sober and was particularly hard hit by the loss of Cory Monteith, her young costar on *Glee*, who died of a drug and alcohol overdose in 2013. Monteith, who played Finn Hudson, the football quarterback and glee club member, was only thirty-one years old when he died and had been dealing with addiction issues since his teens.

During the 2013 Emmy Awards, Lynch paid tribute to Monteith, calling him "a beautiful soul" with a sweet and lovable nature. She also acknowledged his issues with drugs and alcohol and called his death "a tragic reminder of the rapacious, senseless destruction that is brought on by addiction."

After Monteith's death, Lynch and other cast members of *Glee* recorded a public service announcement (PSA) for the Substance Abuse and Mental Health Services Administration (SAMHSA), encouraging people to seek help for their addictions. Lynch reminds viewers that addiction can affect anyone, even someone as successful as Cory Monteith. The title of the PSA was "Our Friend."

smoked marijuana in the past, the drug had made her feel paranoid, but she wanted to be part of the crowd so she smoked, too, which only made her feel worse. Devastated at having given up her sobriety (not counting the over-the-counter medications) just for a chance to be part of the crowd, she called Alcoholics Anonymous (AA) the next morning.

ALCOHOLICS ANONYMOUS

In 1935, a man named Bill Wilson founded Alcoholics Anonymous. An alcoholic himself, Wilson created the twelve steps, the rules that form the bedrock of AA. Spiritually

Members attend an Alcoholics Anonymous meeting. In 1935, an alcoholic named Bill Wilson founded Alcoholics Anonymous and created the twelve steps that are the basis of the program.

based (for example, step two states that the alcoholic "came to believe that a Power greater than ourselves could restore us to sanity"), the steps emphasize taking stock of one's shortcomings, asking for help to overcome them, and trying to make things right with those harmed by actions one took while under the influence of alcohol.

Lynch went to her first AA meeting in January 1992 and took to the program immediately. As someone who liked clear boundaries, she appreciated the structure of the twelve steps and was inspired by the "drunkalogues"—the stories other alcoholics told of their struggles with substance abuse. Given the horrors that some of the other alcoholics had lived through—losing their jobs and families and health—Lynch knew she had been lucky. As she recounts in *Happy Accidents*, she was still able to relate to the feelings of "alienation, self-contempt, and obsession" that her fellow alcoholics discussed, and she would sometimes attend more than one meeting per day.

In an attempt to live a healthier lifestyle, Lynch began doing yoga. It was here that she got to know Laura Coyle, who would become her best friend. Afraid of rejection, Lynch would usually strike first, ending friendships before she could be dumped. Coyle saw through this pattern and made it clear that she wasn't going anywhere, even after the two had a huge fight. Lynch credits Coyle for helping her understand that relationships built on trust could survive arguments and hurt feelings.

After *The Real Live Brady Bunch* finished its run in New York, the creators moved the production to Los Angeles, California. Armed with her new-found sobriety and $10,000—all the money she had in the world—Lynch followed the production to Hollywood.

CHAPTER 4

HOORAY FOR HOLLYWOOD

When Jane Lynch received her star on the Hollywood Walk of Fame in 2013, she gave a speech in which she talked about visiting the same street in 1992 looking for Greta Garbo's star, as the actress was one of Lynch's idols. She then wondered if maybe fifty years in the future history would repeat itself and some young hopeful from a small town would come to Hollywood Boulevard in search of her star.

Lynch now calls Los Angeles home and works for several local charities, including the L.A. Gay and Lesbian Center. According to its website, the center "has been building the health, advocating for the rights and enriching the lives of lesbian, gay, bisexual and transgender people" since 1971.

In 2010, Lynch received the Rand Schrader Distinguished Achievement Award from the Center. Ryan Murphy, the creator of *Glee*, spoke at the event and said that his pride in Lynch knew no bounds

Lynch idolized Greta Garbo, the Swedish-born movie legend who is pictured here around 1940 and who was nominated for an Academy Award three times.

and that she had reached icon status for those in the LGBTQ community.

Of course, years before receiving that award, Lynch had no idea that she would some day have such an impact on the culture. When she came to Los Angeles to continue playing Carol Brady in *The Real Live Brady Bunch*, she was just following her instinct to say yes to whatever work opportunity came her way.

SENDING A LETTER

Lynch had a routine to follow while performing in *The Real Live Brady Bunch*, but once the show ended for the night, she felt lost and alone. She knew this had a lot to do with how distant she felt from her family, with whom she had not discussed her sexual orientation. When she returned to Illinois for the holidays, the conversations never revolved around Lynch's personal life. Even discussing her sobriety was difficult. She came from a family of heavy drinkers, so the thought of seeking help to stop drinking seemed foreign to them.

It was at an AA meeting in Los Angeles where Lynch met the woman who would become her therapist. When they began working together, the woman asked Lynch to write a letter to her parents explaining her reasons for acting distant and her fear that once they knew she was a lesbian, they would reject her.

The therapist told Lynch she didn't have to send the letter, but after revealing her innermost feelings, she decided to mail it. Lynch was delighted to find out that her family accepted her for who she was. They were just relieved that she wasn't sick because she started off the letter by saying she had an important secret to tell them before getting around to telling them that she was gay.

A BIG BREAK

After *The Real Live Brady Bunch* ended its Los Angeles run, Lynch flew to Chicago to work on a play. While she was there, she stayed with the mother of her good friends Jill and Faith Soloway. Elaine, the mother, as well as Elaine's boyfriend, helped Lynch feel less afraid of the parts of her personality that were a bit darker, which helped deepen her work as an actor. Her time with these nurturing people, as well as attending regular AA meetings, made Lynch feel more open to forming deep connections.

She had a professional breakthrough in Chicago, as well. She was cast in *The Fugitive*, a big-budget Hollywood film starring Harrison Ford. As before, Lynch was taking on a part originally written for a man. She played Dr. Kathy Wahlund. She also resorted to her diva ways at first, arguing about the character's wardrobe before her agent reminded her that she was lucky to get a small role in a major film and should act like it.

In *The Fugitive*, Lynch had the chance to work with Harrison Ford (shown here in a scene from the film), one of Hollywood's top actors.

After *The Fugitive* finished filming, Lynch headed back to Los Angeles. She wanted to take advantage of any work that might come her way once the film opened in fall 1993, and to leave behind a failed romance in Chicago. Although she bought a round-trip ticket that would take her back to Chicago in October of that year, she never used the return ticket. The move to Los Angeles would be a permanent one.

THE AUTHORITY FIGURE

In Los Angeles, Lynch rented an apartment not far from her friend Jill Soloway. It was the first time she really put down roots as an adult, making her apartment a home, rather than just a place to stay. This feeling

Lynch was a frequent guest star on TV and had roles in more than fifty shows, including NBC's long-running hit sitcom *Friends*. Here, as Ellen, Lynch appears in a scene with actors Maggie Wheeler, Matthew Perry, and Courtney Cox Arquette.

of being at home included adopting a rescue kitten that she named Greta after her favorite actress, Greta Garbo. Animals remained a passion for Lynch, and she would go on to do PSAs for the Society for the Prevention of Cruelty to Animals (SPCA) and People for the Ethical Treatment of Animals (PETA).

Lynch continued doing sketch work with her friends from *The Real Live Brady Bunch*, and with the help of a supportive agent, she started getting work as a guest star on TV shows. She played lawyers, detectives, doctors, and other authority figures. Many of these roles were originally written for male actors. Lynch didn't understand what, beyond her height, made others see her as a match for these roles because she did not think of herself as a confident, let alone cocky, person. Playing these tough, sometimes bossy, characters became her specialty, however, and led to steady employment.

Lynch rarely refused a job. She was grateful for the work and was starting to learn how important it was to form meaningful business relationships if she wanted to keep getting acting jobs. In time, she would appear in more than fifty TV shows, including hits such as *Friends*, *Frasier*, and *Gilmore Girls*.

By the late 1990s, Lynch was busy with just about any type of job an actor could do: working as a voice-over artist, doing guest spots on television, and appearing in TV commercials. As it turned out, it was a Frosted Flakes commercial that would end up changing her life.

A GUEST STAR

Jane Lynch was a big fan of writer, director, and actor Christopher Guest. A favorite movie of hers was Guest's *Waiting for Guffman* (1997), a comedy about

Lynch and her *Best in Show* costar Jennifer Coolidge (*right*) became fast friends while they were making the movie, directed by Christopher Guest.

a small-town theater group. Given Guest's standing as a moviemaker, Lynch was surprised to see him directing a commercial, though this was something he did quite frequently.

OH, SISTER, MY SISTER!

In 1998, Lynch put on a one-woman show that she wrote titled *Oh, Sister, My Sister!: Deeply Feminine Tales of the Deep Feminine*. The show poked fun at both the women's movement and the self-help movement, which emphasized individual growth above all else. The fictional host of the show was a reporter turned spiritual guide who had written a book called *Listen to Me I'm Talking to You*.

Another character was a lesbian folksinger who had a different "life partner" every time she came back on stage and sang a song about a former lover called "I Gave You the Gun to Shoot Me." At this point in her life, Lynch was not only confident enough to play a lesbian character but also to make a joke at her own expense, too. "I Gave You the Gun to Shoot Me" had been written as a serious song years earlier to describe Lynch's feelings after a bad breakup. Like the folksinger, Lynch had found it difficult to sustain a relationship for more than a month or two.

The character of the Angry Lady was always upset at what she saw as some slight, such as having fellow bike riders pass her on the right, rather than the left, as one would expect. There were traces of Sue Sylvester (the character she would later play in *Glee*) in this uptight character, who spoke more slowly the more upset she became and couldn't understand why others didn't see the world the way that she did.

During the filming of the commercial, Guest told Lynch that he also made movies. Lynch was well aware of this fact, of course, but she tried to remain calm, as Guest did not seem like someone who appreciated people gushing about his work. When Guest suggested that the two of them might work together again someday, Lynch was thrilled.

In 1999, Lynch ran into Guest at a coffee shop in Beverly Hills. He asked her if she was interested in appearing in his movie titled *Best in Show*, a mockumentary (fake documentary) about the competitive world of dog shows. Lynch couldn't believe her luck when she was cast in the film, which was to be shot in Vancouver, Canada.

In *Best in Show*, released in 2000, Lynch played a dog trainer named Christy Cummings who was romantically involved with a female dog owner married to a much older man. This was Lynch's first big film role and she was playing a lesbian, a fact that might cause her to be "outed" in Hollywood. Far more comfortable with her sexuality than in the past, Lynch did not panic over this possibility. As she says in *Happy Accidents*, "Not bad for a former closet dweller!"

PART OF A COMPANY

As with all of Christopher Guest's films, actors in *Best in Show* didn't work from a script. Guest and Eugene Levy, who both had parts in the film as well, created an outline and background information for each character, and it was up to the actors to flesh

Glee producer Michael Hitchcock (*left*) and film director Christopher Guest attend Lynch's Hollywood Walk of Fame ceremony. Guest spoke at the ceremony and praised Lynch's work in three of his movies.

those characters out so that they made sense within the story. In the film, most of Lynch's scenes were with Jennifer Coolidge, who played her lover, and the two worked well together and became close friends.

Guest did not provide much feedback during filming and would often let a scene go on for a long time, gathering the footage he would use to edit the film to match his directorial vision. After years of work, Lynch had enough confidence in her skills that she didn't need constant pats on the back from Guest. Whatever nervousness she felt, she channeled back into her character, a woman she'd decided was full of anxiety.

Lynch loved being part of Guest's company of actors and would go on to star in two more of his films: *A Mighty Wind* (2003), in which she played an adult film star turned folk singer, and *For Your Consideration* (2006), in which she played an entertainment reporter. Working in Guest's films went a long way toward establishing her reputation as a gifted comic actress.

ACTING LIKE A GROWN-UP

After her initial success in *Best in Show*, Lynch decided that, at age thirty-nine, it was time to move beyond renting an apartment—she was still doing her laundry in a laundromat—and settle down in a home, a step toward acting more like an adult and less like a kid who always turned to others for advice and support.

Lynch bought a house in the Laurel Canyon area of Los Angeles for herself and her growing family of pets, which would come to include two dogs and two cats. She decorated her house, entertained guests, and began to feel at home in her artsy neighborhood. She also decided to stop attending AA meetings, confident she could maintain her sobriety on her own. She continued to be open about her struggles with alcohol, however, believing that her story could serve as a positive example to others.

It was during this time that Lynch started to become more interested in political issues. Like many others, Lynch felt particularly vulnerable after the terrorist attacks on September 11, 2001, and found comfort in watching MSNBC, a network that fell to the left of the political spectrum. Her interest in politics and activism would only continue to grow.

CHAPTER 5

FINDING GLEE

J ane Lynch is an actor who believes in giving her all to any role she's chosen to play. This dedication led to constant work in television, and during the early-to-mid-2000s she guest-starred in shows as diverse as *Arrested Development*, *The X-Files*, and *CSI: Crime Scene Investigation.*

Her film roles were less frequent, but she stood out even in small parts. One such role was her character in Judd Apatow's *The 40-Year-Old Virgin*, starring Steve Carell, an actor she'd known since her days in the Second City. Lynch played the manager of the store where Carell's character works and, upon discovering that he is a virgin, discusses her own romantic past with him.

Lynch appears here at the premiere for *The 40-Year-Old Virgin*, alongside costars Kat Dennings (*left*), Steve Carell, and Nancy Walls, who is also Carell's wife.

As with Christopher Guest's films, much of the Apatow movie was improvised, including the Guatemalan love song that Lynch's character sings to Carell. The song paired a sweet melody with lyrics Lynch had cribbed from her high school Spanish text. One line from the song ("*Cuando arreglan mi cuarto, no encuentro nada*") translates to, "Whenever I clean my room, I can't find anything." Lynch's impassioned singing matched with Carell's dumbfounded expression—he had no idea Lynch was going to sing to him—made the scene an instant classic.

RECURRING ROLES

In 2004, Lynch made her first appearance on *Two and a Half Men*, a hit TV comedy starring Charlie Sheen and Jon Cryer. Lynch played Linda Freeman, a psychiatrist who initially treats Jake, the son of

Lynch celebrates the premiere of season two of *The L Word* with (*left to right*) costars Kelly Lynch (no relation) and Camryn Manheim.

Cryer's character. In her first episode, Freeman tries to explain Jake's behavior to his parents and uncle (Sheen), but ends up admitting that she has no clue as to the root of the boy's problems. "Oh, who am I kidding?" she says. "I've got nothing."

A funny line in itself, the comment is particularly amusing given Lynch's long history of therapy. Even a few years before, it would have been hard to imagine Lynch poking fun at a profession that she herself turned to during times of great distress. She was becoming less and less the dark diva complaining about every scene, line, and fellow actor. Lynch would continue to make occasional appearances as Dr. Freeman, who ended up serving as Charlie's therapist, through 2011.

Lynch's recurring role on *The L Word*, a drama about lesbians living in Los Angeles, brought her great joy. She got to play Joyce Wishnia, a lawyer who championed human rights in general and lesbian rights in particular. As Wishnia, she also got to dress in tailored suits. Wearing these suits reminded Lynch of when she would try on her father's clothes as a child, except now she was actually encouraged to dress in a more manly way. She also realized that she'd had difficulty empathizing with the transgender community because she hadn't been able to accept her own more masculine traits.

In the TV show *Party Down*, Lynch played a catering waiter named Constance Carmell, who talked about her former life as an actor constantly, although she never achieved any level of fame. *Party Down* shot its pilot (a single episode used to sell the show to a network) in 2007, but when the show got picked up, Lynch was only able to appear in nine episodes. The reason? Unlike Constance, Lynch was working on another TV show that would make her more famous than she had ever dreamed.

THE VILLAIN

The TV show *Glee* began as a movie script written by Ian Brennan, who would go on to write most of Sue Sylvester's biting dialogue. Brennan was an actor in New York, and when he got the idea to write a film about his experiences as a member of a show choir (another name for glee club), he bought a copy of *Screenwriting for Dummies* and set to work. Brennan managed to get the script into the hands of Ryan Murphy, who'd created the TV shows *Popular*—on which Lynch had appeared—and *Nip/Tuck*. Murphy loved the script but thought it was too dark in tone and told Brennan that it would work better as a TV show that was more upbeat and focused on the friendships formed in glee club.

The Fox television network bought *Glee*, but the head of the studio thought the show needed a villain. He wanted a character whose main goal was

Lynch posed with cheer-leaders after *Glee* was presented at the "upfronts" for Fox television. The upfronts are where television networks present their upcoming season to advertisers and the press.

to destroy the kids in the glee club, called New Directions, and their leader Will Schuester. As Lynch says in *Happy Accidents*, when Ryan Murphy was given this suggestion by the studio, he announced: "Her name will be Sue Sylvester and she will be played by Jane Lynch."

Lynch states in her memoir that she was sold on the script from the start, especially given that the first words used to describe her character were "Sue Sylvester may or may not have posed for *Penthouse*. She may or may not have been on horse estrogen."

Sue was as much a clown as a villain, her ambition and jealousy so over the top as to be laughable. As head coach of the Cheerios, McKinley High's cheerleading squad, Sylvester lorded her power in whatever way she could, snarling her way through the day.

As mean-spirited as Sue Sylvester was, she had great affection for her sister with Down syndrome and showed great emotion when her sibling passed away. Lynch believed that Sue's soft spot was her desire to help those like her sister, Jean, who were vulnerable and could not easily fight those who would prey upon them.

FINDING FAME

Glee's pilot aired on May 19, 2009, and the show quickly became a cultural touchstone. Its young and talented cast was led by Lea Michele as the ambitious Rachel Berry and Cory Monteith as Finn, the quarterback and glee club member who would become her love interest. Although never a ratings blockbuster, the show was a phenomenon, sparking hits on *Billboard*'s Hot 100 list, concert tours, and fans who referred to themselves as "Gleeks." In its first full season, the show was nominated for nineteen Emmy Awards. Lynch would go on to win the Emmy for Outstanding Supporting Actress in a comedy in 2010 and a Golden Globe in the same category in 2011.

Lynch became far more recognizable than she'd ever been in her career, with people stopping her on the street to say how much they loved her acting. She was able to handle this level of fame because she no

LARA EMBRY'S CUSTODY FIGHT

In the late 1990s, Lara Embry was living in Washington with Kimberly Ryan, her partner at the time. The two women decided to have children, and Ryan gave birth to daughter Chase, while Embry carried daughter Haden. Each woman adopted the girl to whom she had not given birth, which was legal in Washington, so that they both became legal parents of both girls.

The family moved to Florida in 2004, and the two women ended their relationship in 2006. Although they had signed a joint custody agreement, Ryan decided that Embry should no longer be able to see Chase.

Embry took Ryan to court, but the court ruled that the adoption in Washington didn't have to be recognized in Florida, a state that prohibited gay adoption. Embry fought the ruling with the help of the National Center for Lesbian Rights (NCLR), and in 2009, the appeals court agreed that she had every right to be in Chase's life. The fact that Embry and Ryan had been in a same-sex relationship had no bearing on her rights and responsibilities as a parent. In 2010, Florida lifted its ban on gay adoption, which had been the law since 1977.

longer felt dependent on other people's view of her to feel good about herself. "I was no longer dependent on the attention for validation, nor was I unmoved by it," she says in her memoir. She could enjoy her success "and put it in the context of the stronger sense of self I had developed."

Interestingly, Lynch, who had become comfortable with her sexual orientation, achieved her greatest fame playing a bigot who often made antigay remarks. In one episode, Sue calls glee club member Kurt Hummel, who is gay (and played by openly gay actor Chris Colfer) "lady." When Kurt tells her that her words are a form of bullying, she gives him three other choices for nicknames: Porcelain, Gelfling, and Tickle-Me-Doughface. Reluctantly, he chooses Porcelain, leaving his boyfriend, Blaine, to be called "other gay."

Of course, Sylvester is so inappropriate in her comments that she highlights how ridiculous this type of bigotry is, forcing viewers to confront their own acts of prejudice. By inhabiting this character so fully and no longer hiding her own lesbianism, Lynch was finding a way to make a difference to those in the LGBTQ community.

A LOVE MATCH

In 2009, Lynch presented her friend Ilene Chaiken, creator of *The L Word*, with the Voice and Visibility Award from the NCLR, an organization that fights for the legal rights of gays and lesbians. Like Chaiken, Lynch would become a strong supporter of the NCLR, receiving its Vanguard Award in 2012 for being an artist whose example young people could follow.

At the 2009 event honoring Chaiken, Lynch met Lara Embry, who would become her wife. Embry was receiving an award for fighting to have same-sex

Lynch and Lara Embry had a whirlwind romance that led to marriage in 2010. Although the two divorced in 2014, they have remained on good terms.

adoptions that took place in one state legally recognized in other states.

Lynch was drawn to Embry, and the two began an intense romance. Although she was embarrassed by her inability to sustain a long-term relationship in the past, Lynch did not feel judged by Embry. She visited Embry in Florida often and grew close to Embry's daughter Haden, who shared Lynch's love of comedy.

When Embry brought up marriage, Lynch hesitated at first because she had grown up believing that marriage was only for straight people. Embry, who was nearly a decade younger, helped Lynch grow more comfortable with the idea, however, and the two were married in Massachusetts in 2010. The wedding was featured in the widely read *New York Times* Vows column. Embry and her daughter moved to Los Angeles, and Lynch settled into married life and steady work on a wildly popular TV show.

CHAPTER 6

BALANCING ACT

Not long before Jane Lynch started working on *Glee*, she took on a huge challenge, playing opposite Meryl Streep, considered by many to be the best actress of her generation, in the Nora Ephron film *Julie and Julia*. Streep played chef Julia Child and Lynch her sister, Dorothy McWilliams. Lynch was nervous about working with Streep, but she plowed ahead, excited by the opportunity to do a few scenes with such a celebrated actress. When Ephron took Lynch aside to tell her she was doing great work, she was ecstatic.

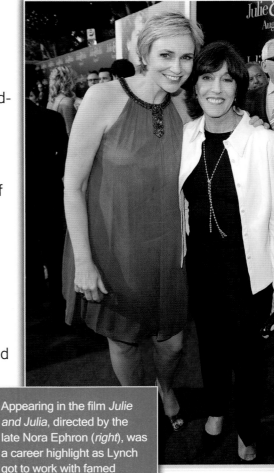

Appearing in the film *Julie and Julia*, directed by the late Nora Ephron (*right*), was a career highlight as Lynch got to work with famed actress Meryl Streep.

At Madame Tussauds in Hollywood, Lynch comes face to face with her wax figurine of herself, dressed in character as *Glee*'s Sue Sylvester.

Glee gave Lynch plenty of chances to stretch her performing muscles, too. The show revolved around musical numbers, and although Lynch was rarely a part of these, she did appear in a salute to Madonna's "Vogue" video.

"I'm not a dancer," Lynch told a reporter at Advocate.com. "I am a woman who knows her limitations. But that doesn't mean I won't work really hard and try. They say you only have to get it right once, and luckily we were rolling the one time I got it right."

In 2010, Lynch had the chance to work with legendary comedian Carol Burnett, a childhood idol, who played Sue's mother, Doris. Doris is a neglectful mother, and Sue "[t]he orphaned, thrown-away child who's forced to fend for herself and her vulnerable sister," Lynch told the *Advocate*. She believed that Sue's background helped explain her tough-as-nails exterior.

That same year, Madame Tussauds museum honored Lynch by having a wax replica of Sue Sylvester added to the collection, alongside wax versions of actors such as Tom Hanks and Halle Berry. Lynch found the experience flattering but bizarre, especially when she saw two workers carrying the figurine away, with one holding Sue's head, and another, her body.

MARRIAGE INEQUALITY

Although Lynch had lived in California for years, she and Embry were not allowed to marry there in 2010 because in November 2008, California voters passed a constitutional amendment, known as Proposition 8 (Prop 8), banning same-sex marriage. According to the *Bay Citizen*, up until that time, an estimated twenty-eight thousand couples had married in the state. A 2009 decision by the California Supreme Court allowed those earlier marriages to remain in effect.

The sponsors of Prop 8 were a group known as ProtectMarriage.com that believed marriage should be the union of one man with one woman.

Groups that believed in marriage equality (the right of same-sex couples to marry) were determined to fight Prop 8, while several religious groups, including the Church of Jesus Christ of Latter Day Saints and the Roman Catholic Church, joined with ProtectMarriage.com to support the measure. Organizations such as Focus on the Family, which describes itself as a Christian ministry, were in favor of Prop 8, too. Jim Daly, president and chief executive officer of Focus on the Family, told National Public Radio that same-sex marriage was "just one of many things that are outside of God's design for human sexuality."

Not surprisingly, Jane Lynch was strongly opposed to Prop 8. In 2010, she expressed her views to the *Guardian*. "Shouldn't there be safeguards against the majority voting on the rights of a minority?" she wondered. "If people voted on civil rights in the '60s, it would never have happened."

A PHOTOGRAPHIC PROTEST

One group protesting Prop 8 was the NOH8 (No Hate) Campaign, which was founded by photographer Adam Bouska and his partner Jeff Parsley. The heart of the campaign was a photographic silent protest. In the photos taken by Bouska, celebrities and average citizens were photographed with duct tape over their mouths to show how Prop 8 and other laws around the world had silenced their voices. Participants also had NOH8 painted on their faces.

Jane Lynch was one of the celebrities to do a NOH8 photograph, along with others such as Josh Hutcherson, the Kardashians, and fellow *Glee* stars Kevin McHale and Jenna Ushkowitz. As of January 2014, there were more than thirty-four thousand photographs on the NOH8 website. Adam Bouska also shot the cover photo of Lynch's memoir, *Happy Accidents*.

Lynch's memoir *Happy Accidents*, published in 2011, is an honest account of both the actress's struggles and successes on her way to fame.

THE SUPREME COURT RULES

Lynch participated in the play *8* by Dustin Lance
Black, which was based on transcripts from the initial

On March 26, 2013, these demonstrators showed support for same-sex marriage while the Supreme Court heard legal arguments both for and against California's Proposition 8.

federal trial to strike down Prop 8. She portrayed Maggie Gallagher, a vocal opponent of same-sex marriage, and her performance opposite activist Cleve Jones, who played marriage equality advocate Evan Wolfson, was a highlight of the play. The play raised more than $2 million to support marriage equality.

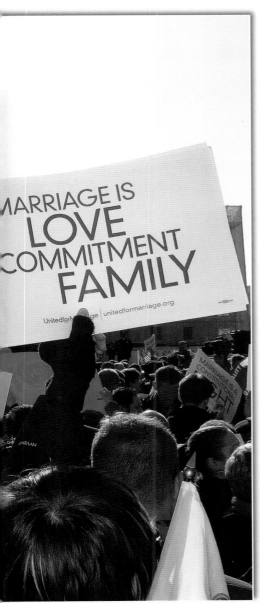

In 2010, Judge Vaughn Walker ruled to strike down Prop 8, but this was not the end of the legal battle. The case went all the way to the Supreme Court, the highest court in the United States. On June 26, 2013, the Supreme Court ruled against ProtectMarriage.com, the sponsors of Prop 8. The justices didn't rule on whether gay marriage was a constitutional right, however. Instead it stated that ProtectMarriage.com, a private organization, didn't have the right to sue simply because it didn't like the idea of same-sex couples getting married.

This narrow ruling meant that gay marriage was legal again in California, but other states did not have to follow their lead. However, in the year following the ruling, the number of states that legalized gay marriage jumped from nine to nineteen, plus the District of Columbia, while thirty-one states still banned gay marriage.

A federal judge in Utah overturned the ban on gay marriage in that state in December 2013, but same-sex marriage was put on hold—called a stay—as the state appealed the decision. This is based on a January 2014 Supreme Court ruling that no more same-sex couples could marry in Utah until the appeal was heard by the United States Court of Appeals for that district. As in the Prop 8 case, the Supreme Court did not rule on whether gay couples had the same right to marry as straight couples, but simply put a stay on those marriages. Despite this ruling, U.S. Attorney General Eric Holder stated that the federal government would recognize the more than one thousand marriages that had already taken place in Utah as legal.

Judges in other states have ruled the ban on gay marriage unconstitutional, but with the exception of Pennsylvania, a state in which the governor did not appeal the decision, these judges put same-sex marriage on hold as each state went through the appeals process. Gay marriage is a rapidly evolving issue, and most legal analysts expect the Supreme Court will to have to tackle it head on in the not-too-distant future.

THE DEFENSE OF MARRIAGE ACT

In June 2013, the Supreme Court ruled on another major case affecting the LGBTQ community. Back in 1996, President Bill Clinton signed a federal law called the Defense of Marriage Act (DOMA) that defined marriage as between a man and a woman. *United States v. Windsor*, the case before the Supreme Court, concerned a woman named Edith Windsor who had inherited a large sum of money from her late wife. Windsor was forced to pay more than $300,000 in estate taxes, which she would not have had to pay if either she or her deceased spouse were male because the U.S. government didn't view her marriage as legal.

The court struck down a key part of DOMA, ruling that it was unconstitutional for the terms "spouse" and "marriage" to apply only to heterosexual couples. This change affected not just taxes, but also Social Security benefits, military benefits, and retirement benefits.

The *Windsor* ruling did not mean that every state had to recognize same-sex marriages, only that the federal government had to recognize marriages in states where those unions were already legal. In January 2014, however, the federal government expanded the law, giving federal benefits to married same-sex couples even if they lived in a state that did not allow gay marriage.

A PRESIDENT'S SUPPORT

President Barack Obama was the first president to come out in favor of marriage equality while still in office. On May 9, 2012, he gave an interview with

In this photo Lynch (*far right*), who hosted the 2013 Christmas tree lighting ceremony at the White House, celebrates the event with President Barack Obama, singer Joshua Bell (*left, in black suit*), opera star Renée Fleming (*left, in white coat*), pop star Mariah Carey (*right, in white*), and others.

ABC News reporter Robin Roberts in which he stated his support of gay marriage. "It is important for me to go ahead and affirm that I think same-sex couples should be able to get married," he told Roberts.

During the interview, Obama highlighted the impact that young people were having on this issue, stating that even when he met college students who disagreed with him on many issues, "when it comes to same-sex equality, or sexual orientation, they believe in equality."

Lynch was thrilled about President Obama's support. During an appearance on *The Rachel Maddow Show* later that month, she said that she was touched by Obama's declaration. She admitted that, although she had worked for marriage equality, she felt emotionally removed from the issue at times. Obama's comments had affected her greatly, however, and helped her redouble her efforts for the cause.

Lynch would go on to host fund-raisers for the president and to provide the voice-over narration for a reelection video aimed at the LGBTQ community. She even hosted the National Tree Lighting ceremony at the White House in December 2013.

STANDING UP FOR OTHERS

As Jane Lynch's fame has grown, she has used her visibility to support causes close to her heart. In May 2012, she did a PSA with Lauren Potter, an actress with Down syndrome who plays Becky, Sue Sylvester's sidekick and "becretary" on *Glee*. Titled "Not Acceptable," the PSA, part of the Spread the Word to End the Word campaign, is a reminder that using the word "retarded" as an everyday term is the same as using any minority slur and should be seen as equally unacceptable.

The same year, Lynch, whose character on *Glee* is the sister and mother of someone with Down syndrome, was honored by the National Down Syndrome Society. In a video message taped for the event, Potter said of Lynch, "The world would be a better place if more people saw beauty the way you do and chose to recognize abilities, rather than disabilities."

Project Angel Food, a Los Angeles–based charity that cooks

and delivers meals to people dealing with HIV/AIDs, cancer, and other serious illnesses, is another organization that Lynch supports. She received Project Angel Food's Angel Award in December 2013, and during

Lynch hosts the Trevor Project's TrevorLIVE event in June 2013. Later that year, she received the organization's Hero Award for her work in support of LGBTQ youth.

her acceptance speech she emphasized the importance of providing food for others. "It's such a simple act, and it's so powerful that it shoots love and light into the cells of everyone involved," she said.

Lynch has also hosted TrevorLIVE, a fund-raising event for the Trevor Project, which provides crisis intervention and suicide prevention services for LGBTQ youths. In December 2013, Lynch received the Trevor Hero Award at an event in Los Angeles for her work with the organization. Many cast members of *Glee* were present to honor Lynch, a testament to how well liked she is by her fellow actors.

IN FULL BLOOM

Jane Lynch continues to thrive professionally and personally. Although she and Lara Embry separated in 2013 and divorced in January 2014, Lynch emphasized that the two remained on good terms. Lynch was proud that she and Embry had acted in a mature way, putting the needs of Embry's daughter Haden first. Although it took some time to work out the financial aspects of the divorce settlement, the former couple even spent part of the 2013 holiday season together.

Glee continues to offer Lynch a meaty role to play. Still sarcastic and mean-spirited (she stole Principal Figgins's job by planting X-rated material in his office and uses her power to shut down the glee club for good), Sue continues to show her vulnerability, too. When Becky says that she wants to go to college, for example, Sue is unsupportive at first. After realizing how happy the idea makes Becky, however, Sue says that while she will miss her "becretary" terribly, the girl should move on. Sue also deals with feelings of inadequacy when a school board member mistakes her for a man. This misunderstanding is an interesting echo of Lynch's own life as someone who has often played roles intended for men and has worked to feel comfortable with the more masculine side of her personality.

Lynch has had the chance to return to the stage playing *Annie*'s Miss Hannigan on Broadway and the chance to charm audiences as the host of *Hollywood Game Night*, a show where celebrities play different party games. Although her greatest success came later in life—she was forty-nine when *Glee* began—Lynch is clearly enjoying her career and the opportunities it provides her, including the opportunity to give back to others. As Bill Keveney of *USA Today* puts it, "Jane Lynch might be considered a bit of a late bloomer. But what a bloom."

T I M E L I N E

1960 Jane Marie Lynch born on July 14 in Dolton, Illinois.

1978 Lynch appears in high school production of *Godspell*.

1982 Lynch graduates from Illinois State University and begins master's program in theater at Cornell University.

1984 Lynch moves to New York City to begin professional acting career.

1985 Lynch returns to Illinois after an unsuccessful nine months in New York City.

1987 Lynch starts working in the touring company of the Second City, a sketch comedy group.

1990 Lynch takes role as Carol Brady in *The Real Live Brady Bunch* in Chicago.

1992 Lynch joins Alcoholics Anonymous (AA).

1993 Lynch has a small role in *The Fugitive* opposite Harrison Ford and moves to Los Angeles on a permanent basis.

1995 Lynch begins her long stint doing guest spots on TV with roles on shows such as *Friends* and *Gilmore Girls.*

1998 Lynch's one-woman show *Oh, Sister, My Sister!* opens in Los Angeles.

1999 Lynch moves to her first house in the Laurel Canyon section of Los Angeles.

2000 Lynch appears in Christopher Guest's *Best in Show*.

2003 Lynch's father, Frank, dies on June 11.

2004 Lynch makes her first appearance as Dr. Linda Freeman on *Two and a Half Men*.

2005 Lynch has a breakout role opposite Steve Carell in *The 40-Year-Old Virgin* and makes her first appearance in *The L Word*.

2006 Lynch appears in two comedies: Guest's *For Your Consideration* and *Talladega Nights* starring Will Ferrell.

2008 Lynch starts shooting *Julie and Julia*, opposite Meryl Streep.

2009 Lynch begins her run as Sue Sylvester in the pilot of *Glee*. She meets Lara Embry at an evening honoring *The L Word* creator Ilene Chaiken.

2010 Lynch and Embry marry in Massachusetts on May 31st. Lynch wins an Emmy for Outstanding Supporting Actress for *Glee* and is honored by Madame Tussauds museum, which makes a wax figure of Lynch as Sue Sylvester.

2011 Lynch wins a Golden Globe Award for supporting actress and hosts the 63rd Annual Emmy Awards.

2012 Lynch's mother, Eileen, passes away on January 30. Lynch appears in *8*, Dustin Lance Black's play about the fight for marriage equality.

2013 Lynch and Embry separate and file for divorce. Lynch receives awards for her work with Project Angel Food and the Trevor Project.

2014 Lynch's divorce becomes final in January. Lynch hosts the 66th Annual Directors Guild Awards. She joins the Ban Bossy campaign, which encourages girls to take leadership roles in their community. She also performs a cabaret show at 54 Below, a theater in New York City, and publishes *Marlene Marlene, Queen of Mean*, a children's picture book.

GLOSSARY

ACTIVIST Someone who acts on behalf of a certain cause, particularly a political one.

ADVOCATING Offering public support of a policy, cause, or group of people.

AMENDMENT A formal change or addition to a legal document such as a state's constitution.

DISCRIMINATION Treating people unfairly based on their race, religion, or sexual orientation.

EMPATHIZING Showing an understanding of and compassion toward another person's feelings and experience.

EQUANIMITY The ability to remain calm and even-tempered, especially when dealing with new or difficult circumstances.

FUNDAMENTAL That which is most basic or essential about an idea or situation.

HARASSMENT The creation of an uncomfortable or hostile situation through words and actions.

IMPASSIONED Filled with a great amount of intense emotion.

INTEGRATED Including people from different racial, religious, or ethnic backgrounds.

IRRATIONAL Thinking in an unclear, illogical, or unreasonable way.

MEMOIR A written account of the author's personal experience, usually set within a certain time frame.

NEGLECTFUL Not treating someone or something with the proper amount of attention and concern.

RAPACIOUS Extremely greedy to the point of preying on others to satisfy a need.

REENACTMENT A performance that recreates an event that already took place at an earlier time.

SEXUAL ORIENTATION A pattern of emotional, romantic, or sexual attraction toward members of the same, opposite, or both sexes.

SLUR A mean comment about another person meant to hurt his or her feelings or reputation.

SOBRIETY The condition in which a person addicted to alcohol or drugs is sober, meaning he or she no longer drinks or uses drugs.

TRANSGENDER Feeling that one's gender identity and expression does not match the sex with which he or she was born.

TURMOIL An extremely upset, confused, or disturbed condition.

Egale Canada Human Rights Trust (ECHRT)
185 Carlton Street
Toronto, ON M5A 2K7
Canada
(888) 204-7777
Website: http://www.egale.ca
ECHRT promotes the rights of the LGBT community
and offers resources to help maintain safer
schools for LGBT youth and prevent discrimination based on sexual orientation.

Human Rights Campaign (HRC)
1640 Rhode Island Avenue NW
Washington, DC 20036-3278
(800) 777-4723
Website: http://www.hrc.org
The Human Rights Campaign is the largest national
organization fighting for equal rights for the
LGBT community. Its website provides information on marriage equality, workplace rights, and
civil rights for those oppressed because of their
sexual orientation.

It Gets Better Project
110 South Fairfax Avenue
Suite A11-71
Los Angeles, CA 90036
Website: http://www.itgetsbetter.org

The It Gets Better Project was created to offer
messages of hope for LGBT teens facing bullying. There are more than fifty thousand videos
on the site, with politicians, celebrities, and
everyday people reassuring youths that their
lives will get better as they move beyond their
teen years.

National Center for Lesbian Rights (NCLR)
870 Market Street, Suite 370
San Francisco, CA 94102
(415) 392-6257
Website: http://www.nclrights.org
The National Center for Lesbian Rights advocates for
the LGBT community and offers resources for
those involved in custody disputes, immigration
issues, and other legal matters.

Supporting Our Youth (SOY)
333 Sherbourne Street, 2nd Floor
Toronto, ON M5A 2S5
Canada
(416) 324-5077
Website: http://www.soytoronto.org
Supporting Our Youth provides healthy arts, culture,
and recreational spaces for young people, as well
as housing and employment opportunities and
access to mentoring and support.

The Trevor Project
P.O. Box 69232
West Hollywood, CA 90069
(866) 488-7386
Website: http://www.thetrevorproject.org
The Trevor Project provides crisis intervention and
    suicide prevention services to lesbian, gay, bisex-
    ual, transgender, and questioning (LGBTQ) young
    people. The project operates TrevorSpace, a social
    networking site for LGBTQ youth.

WEBSITES

Because of the changing nature of Internet links,
Rosen Publishing has developed an online list of
websites related to the subject of this book. This site
is updated regularly. Please use this link to access
the list:

http://www.rosenlinks.com/LGBT/Lynch

Belge, Kathy, and Marke Bieschke. *Queer: The Ultimate LGBT Guide for Teens.* Milton Keynes, England: Zest Publishing, 2011.

Bernstein, Mary, and Verta Taylor, eds. *The Marrying Kind? Debating Same-Sex Marriage Within the Lesbian and Gay Movement.* Minneapolis, MN: University of Minnesota Press, 2013.

Bigelow, Lisa Jenn. *Starting from Here.* N.p.: Amazon Publishing, 2012.

Boylan, Jennifer Finney. *She's Not There: A Life in Two Genders.* Rev. ed. New York, NY: Broadway Books, 2013.

Bronski, Michael, Ann Pellegrini, and Michael Amico. *"You Can Tell Just by Looking": And 20 Other Myths About LGBT Life and People.* Boston, MA: Beacon Press, 2013.

Burgess, Susan. *The New York Times on Gay and Lesbian Issues.* Thousand Oaks, CA: CQ Press, 2011.

Cartlidge, Cherese. *Neil Patrick Harris.* Farmington Hills, MI: Lucent Books, 2011.

Danforth, Emily. *The Miseducation of Cameron Post.* New York, NY: Balzer & Bray, 2013.

DeGeneres, Ellen. *Seriously...I'm Kidding.* New York, NY: Grand Central Publishing, 2011.

Ehrensaft, Diane. *Gender Born, Gender Made: Raising Healthy Gender-Nonconforming Children.* New York, NY: The Experiment, 2011.

Huegel, Kelly. *GLBTQ: The Survival Guide for Gay, Lesbian, Bisexual, Transgender, and Questioning Teens.* Minneapolis, MN: Free Spirit Publishing, 2011.

Konigsberg, Bill. *Openly Straight.* New York, NY: Arthur A. Levine Books, 2013.

LaSala, Michael C. *Coming Out, Coming Home: Helping Families Adjust to a Gay or Lesbian Child.* New York, NY: Columbia University Press, 2010.

Martin, Ricky. *Me.* New York, NY: Celebra, 2010.

Moon, Sarah, and James Lecesne, eds. *The Letter Q: Queer Writers' Notes to Their Younger Selves.* New York, NY: Arthur A. Levine Books, 2012.

Nagle, Jeanne. *GLBT Teens and Society* (Teens: Being Gay, Lesbian, Bisexual, or Transgender). New York, NY: Rosen Publishing, 2010.

Orr, Tamra B. *Home and Family Relationships* (Teens: Being Gay, Lesbian, Bisexual, or Transgender). New York, NY: Rosen Publishing, 2010.

Payment, Simone. *Friendship, Dating, and Relationships* (Teens: Being Gay, Lesbian, Bisexual, or Transgender). New York, NY: Rosen Publishing, 2010.

Savage, Dan, and Terry Miller, eds. *It Gets Better: Coming Out, Overcoming Bullying, and Creating a Life Worth Living.* New York, NY: Plume, 2012.

Schwartz, John. *Oddly Normal: One Family's Struggle to Help Their Teenage Son Come to Terms with His Sexuality.* New York, NY: Gotham Books, 2013.

Shelton, Michael. *Family Pride: What LGBT Families Should Know About Navigating Home, School, and Safety in Their Neighborhoods.* Boston, MA: Beacon Press, 2013.

Wahls, Zach. *My Two Moms: Lessons of Love, Strength, and What Makes a Family.* New York, NY: Gotham Books, 2013.

Winterson, Jeannette. *Why Be Happy When You Could Be Normal?* New York, NY: Grove Press, 2012.

Worth, Richard. *Life at School and in the Community* (Teens: Being Gay, Lesbian, Bisexual, or Transgender). New York, NY: Rosen Publishing, 2010.

Anderson-Minshall, Diane. "Jane Lynch and the Mommy Track (Suit)." Advocate.com, September 12, 2011. Retrieved December 12, 2013 (http://www.advocate .com/arts-entertainment/television/2011/09/12/jane -lynch-and-mommy-track-suit).

Apatow, Judd, and Steve Carell. *The 40-Year-Old Virgin.* Universal City, CA: Universal Studios, 2005.

Gast, Phil. "Obama Announces He Supports Same-Sex Marriage." CNN Politics, May 9, 2012. Retrieved December 15, 2013 (http://www.cnn.com/2012/ 05/09/politics/obama-same-sex-marriage).

Goldman, Andrew. "See Jane Run." *Elle*, January 24, 2011. Retrieved December 5, 2012 (http://www .elle.com/pop-culture/celebrities/see-jane-run-2).

Human Rights Campaign. "Mission Statement." Retrieved December 10, 2013 (http://www.hrc .org/the-hrc-story/mission-statement).

It Gets Better Project. "President Obama: It Gets Better." Retrieved November 26, 2013 (http:// www.itgetsbetter.org/video/entry/geyafbsdpvk).

It Gets Better Project. "White House Staff: It Gets Better." Retrieved November 26, 2013 (http:// www.itgetsbetter.org/video/entry/2610).

Jensen, Michael. "Jane Lynch Says Straight Audiences Not Ready for Gay Actors in Leading Roles." *The Backlot*, January 12, 2011. Retrieved December 15, 2013 (http://www.thebacklot.com/jane-lynch-says -straight-audiences-not-ready-for-gay-actors-in -leading-roles/01/2011/).

Lorre, Chuck, Lee Aronsohn, Jeff Abugov, and Mark
     Roberts. "Hey, Can I Pee Outside in the Dark?" *Two
     and a Half Men*, season 1, episode 20. Aired April
     19, 2004.

Lynch, Jane. "Bill of Rights Award Speech."
     YouTube video, from an appearance at the ACLU of
     Southern California Bill of Rights Awards. Retrieved
     December 2, 2013 (http://www.youtube.com/
     watch?v=Everf-eBPX4).

Lynch, Jane. *Happy Accidents*. New York, NY:
     Hyperion, 2011.

Lynch, Jane. "Human Rights Campaign National Dinner
     Speech." YouTube video, from an appearance at the
     Human Rights Campaign National Dinner, October
     10, 2009. Retrieved November 20, 2013 (http://
     www.youtube.com/watch?v=H9z3YSGLwhc).

Lynch, Jane. Interview with Joy Behar. YouTube video,
     from an appearance on *The Joy Behar Show*,
     September 15, 2011. Retrieved November 22, 2013
     (http://www.youtube.com/watch?v=OML4-GWkM3g).

Mullins, Jenna. "Cory Monteith's Emmy Tribute." E!
     Online, September 22, 2013. Retrieved December
     5, 2013 (http://www.eonline.com/news/461648/
     cory-monteith-s-emmy-tribute-jane-lynch-honors
     -her-gifted-and-wonderful-glee-costar).

Murphy, Ryan. "Furt." *Glee*, season 2, episode 8.
     Aired November 23, 2010.

Newman, Judith. "Jane Lynch Finds Herself." *New York
     Times*, September 16, 2011. Retrieved December

2, 2013 (http://www.nytimes.com/2011/09/
18/fashion/jane-lynch-finds-herself.html
?pagewanted=all).

Olivier, Ellen. "Angel Awards for Jane Lynch and
Giada De Laurentiis." *Society News LA*, August
11, 2013. Retrieved December 19, 2013 (http://
societynewsla.com/angel-awards-for-jane-lynch
-and-giada-de-laurentiis).

Pew Research Global Attitudes Project. "The Global
Divide on Homosexuality." June 4, 2013. Retrieved
November 24, 2013 (http://www.pewglobal.org/
2013/06/04/the-global-divide-on-homosexuality).

Potter, Lauren. "Video Message at the NDSS 2012
Spring Luncheon." YouTube video, June 6, 2012.
Retrieved January 4, 2014 (http://www.youtube
.com/watch?v=uMyUU3AZxns).

Rochlin, Margy. "Jane Lynch's Year of Living
Famously." *More*, November 2010. Retrieved
December 2, 2013 (http://www.more.com/news/
womens-issues/jane-lynchs-year-living-famously).

Smith College. "2012 Commencement Address by
Jane Lynch." May 20, 2012. Retrieved December
3, 2013 (http://www.smith.edu/events
/commencement_speech2012.php).

ABOUT THE AUTHOR

Jennifer Landau received her MA degree in creative writing from New York University and her MST in general and special education from Fordham University. Landau has been a fan of Jane Lynch's work since seeing Lynch's performance in *Best in Show*. Besides being an experienced editor, Landau has written nonfiction books, including *The Right Words: Knowing What to Say and How to Say It*; *Jeff Bezos and Amazon*; and *Cybercitizenship: Online Rights and Responsibilities*.

PHOTO CREDITS

Cover, p. 23 David Livingston/Getty Images; pp. 6–7 Amanda Edwards/WireImage/Getty Images; pp. 10–11 nationalatlas.gov; pp. 12–13 Smith College/AP Images; pp. 16–17 Chris Pizzello/ Invision/AP Images; p. 18 Keystone/Hulton Archive/Getty Images; pp. 24–25 Bennett Raglin/WireImage/Getty Images; p. 27 Jonathan Leibson/Getty Images; p. 32 Warner Bros./Moviepix/Getty Images; pp. 34–35 Kenneth C. Zirkel/E+/Getty Images; p. 37 Sara Krulwich/ The New York Times/Redux; pp. 40–41 Michael Stuparyk/Toronto Star/Getty Images; pp. 42–43 Paul Natkin/WireImage/Getty Images; p. 46 New York Daily News Archive/Getty Images; pp. 48–49 Hank Morgan/Photo Researchers/Getty Images; p. 53 Silver Screen Collection/Moviepix/Getty Images; pp. 56–57 Archive Photos/ Moviepix/Getty Images; pp. 58–59, 60–61 Warner Bros./Photofest; pp. 64–65 Dan Steinberg/Invision/AP Images; pp. 68–69, 79, 81 Kevin Winter/Getty Images; pp. 70–71 Jean-Paul Aussenard/ WireImage/Getty Images; pp. 74–75, 86–87, 90–91 © AP Images; p. 82 Gabriel Bouys/AFP/Getty Images; p. 85 Michael N. Todaro/ Getty Images; pp. 92–93 Stephen Lovekin/Getty Images; cover and interior graphic elements © iStockphoto.com/traffic_analyzer (colored stripes), © iStockphoto.com/rusm (pebbled texture).

Designer: Nicole Russo; Editor: Kathy Kuhtz Campbell; Photo Researcher: Marty Levick